The Greatest Bible Stories Ever Told
Prayer & Promise

Stephen Elkins
AUTHOR

Tim O'Connor
ILLUSTRATIONS

BROADMAN
& HOLMAN
PUBLISHERS

NASHVILLE, TENNESSEE

Copyright © 1999 by Stephen Elkins / Wonder Workshop, Inc.
Published in 2002 by Broadman & Holman Publishers
Nashville, Tennessee

Scripture quotations on pages 3, 10, 16, 24, 25, 26, 27, 28, and 29 are from the HOLY BIBLE, NEW INTERNATIONAL VERSION®, copyright © 1973, 1978, 1984 by International Bible Society. Used by permission of Zondervan Publishing House. All rights reserved.

Scripture quotation on pages 9 and 30 are from the New American Standard Bible, © the Lockman Foundation, 1960, 1962, 1963, 1971, 1972, 1973, 1975, 1977; used by permission.

Scripture quotations on pages 14 and 20 are from the King James Version.

All songs (except Public Domain) written, adapted, and/or arranged by Stephen Elkins, © 1999 Wonder Workshop, Inc. All rights reserved. International copyright secured.

Cover design and layout by Bill Farrar

A catalog record for the original Word & Song Bible is available from the Library of Congress.

All rights reserved. Printed in Belgium.

ISBN 0-8054-2472-5

1 2 3 4 5   06 05 04 03 02

DANIEL AND THE LIONS' DEN

Daniel 6:27 (God) rescues and he saves; he performs signs and wonders.

In the third year of the reign of King Jehoiakim, Jerusalem was attacked and defeated by King Nebuchadnezzar of Babylon. The Babylonians carried off the cups and other vessels from the holy temple. They began using them in their own idol worship.

The king then ordered the smartest and most handsome young men of Israel to be brought to his palace. There they would stay for three years being trained to serve the king.

One of these young men was a Jewish boy named Daniel.

Each day Daniel was given a portion of royal food and wine, but he refused to eat it. He chose instead to eat vegetables and drink water. In doing so, he did not break the Jewish law.

When the three years of training ended, all of the young men were presented to King Nebuchadnezzar. Daniel was by far the smartest and most handsome of them all. That day, he entered the king's service.

He served for many years until Nebuchadnezzar died and his grandson Belshazzar became king.

The Lord gave Daniel the gift of interpreting dreams. On many occasions, Daniel was able to interpret the king's dreams and he soon became well-known as a very wise man of God. One night, Belshazzar gave a great party. A thousand guests were there. The king gave orders to bring out the gold and silver cups stolen from the Jewish temple years ago. They began pouring wine into these holy cups while they praised their false gods. The Lord was very angry. Suddenly, a mysterious hand appeared in the room and began writing strange words on the palace wall.

The king collapsed with fear. He called out, "If anyone can tell me what this means, speak now and I will make you third in command of Babylon." All of the king's wise men tried, but they could not read the message. Then the queen spoke, "There is a man who walks with the God of Israel in your kingdom. His name is Daniel. Call for him. He will tell you what the writing means."

So Daniel was brought before the king. "Can you read this? Tell me!" demanded the king. "Yes, O king. God has given me the ability to read it," answered Daniel. "It says you have not honored the living God, but mocked Him."

Daniel was made third in command of Babylon. But that night Belshazzar, king of Babylon was killed and Darius the Mede took over the kingdom.

King Darius hand-picked 120 princes to rule his new kingdom. He then selected three presidents to oversee the princes. Of these three, Daniel became the most important.

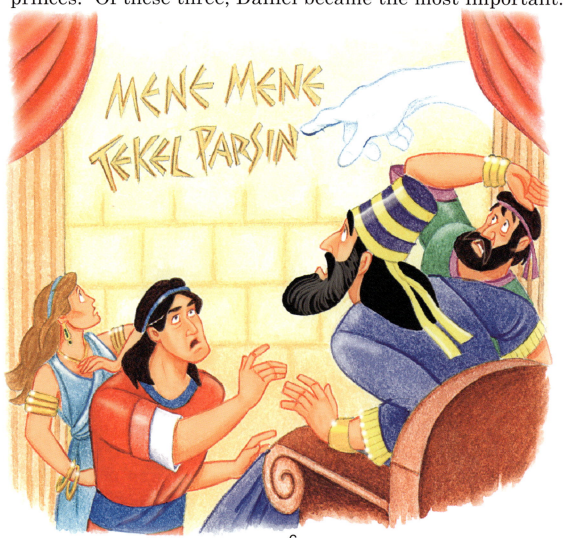

The other presidents and governors were jealous that Daniel had been honored in this way, so they plotted against him.

They went to the king as a group and said, "O King Darius, all of us have agreed that you should make a new law this day; a law that will unite the kingdom. The new law would make it a crime for anyone to pray to any god or man but you, O king, for the next thirty days. And if anyone should break the new law, they would be thrown into the lions' den." So King Darius agreed and it was put into writing.

Now when Daniel heard about the new law, he went upstairs to his room, got down on his knees, and prayed, just as he had done before. When the princes and governors found Daniel praying, they ran to the king and said, "Daniel has broken your new law, O king. He must be punished. Throw him to the lions!" Darius did not want to harm Daniel, but these evil men had tricked him. So King Darius gave the order, "Put Daniel into the lions' den."

They took Daniel to the lions' den and threw him in. Then King Darius spoke to Daniel, "May the God whom you serve rescue you!" Then they sealed the den shut and the king returned to the palace.

At dawn, the king arose from a sleepless night and hurried to the den. "Daniel," he cried, "are you alive? Has your God rescued you from the lions?" Daniel answered, "My God has sent an angel who shut the mouths of the lions. They have not hurt me, nor have I done any wrong to you, O king."

"Pull him up!" shouted the king. Then, at the king's command, those men who had falsely accused Daniel were thrown into the den of lions. Then King Darius sent a letter throughout the kingdom which read: All of the people of the kingdom must fear and respect the God of Daniel, for He is the living God who rescued and saved Daniel from the lions.

Daniel loved the Lord and faithfully served Him.

Affirmation: I will honor the living God!

EVERY DAY IS PRAY DAY!

1 Thessalonians 5:16-18 Rejoice always; pray without ceasing, (and) in everything give thanks.

Paul had a great love and pleasant memories of the church in Thessalonica. Their faith and love of God had grown even while they were being treated very harshly. They shared the Word of God with others and they lived it every day. They believed, as we do, that Jesus is alive and someday He is coming back to this earth to claim us as His people. Because of this wonderful news, Paul writes, "Rejoice always, pray without ceasing, and in everything give thanks!"

Affirmation: I will rejoice and pray!

JACOB'S STAIRWAY TO HEAVEN

Genesis 28:15 (Behold) I am with you and will watch over you.

Isaac and Rebekah had twin sons named Jacob and Esau. Esau was born first and rightly deserved the blessings given to the oldest son. But Jacob, who was very clever, tricked Isaac into giving the blessing to him. When Esau discovered what his younger brother had done he said, "The day is coming when I will kill Jacob."

When Rebekah heard what Esau had said, she sent for Jacob and told him to leave at once. "You must go to my brother Laban's house in Haran. Stay there until Esau's anger is quieted."

Rebekah told her husband that Jacob was going to Haran to find a godly wife. So Isaac blessed him with the blessings of Abraham and sent him on his way.

One evening on the way to Haran, Jacob stopped to rest for the night. He spread his blanket across the ground and used a large stone for a pillow. He fell asleep and dreamed he saw a stairway to heaven. The bottom of the stairway rested on the earth, the top reached to heaven. And the angels of God were climbing up and down the heavenly stairway.

There above the stairway stood Yahweh, our Lord, and He said, "I am the Lord the God of Abraham, your grandfather, and the God of Isaac, your father. I make this promise to you. I will give to you and your children this land where you are now sleeping. All the people on earth will be blessed because of you and your family. I will watch over you and no matter where you go, I will be with you."

Jacob woke up frightened. "Surely the presence of the Lord is in this place and I didn't know it," he said. So early the next morning Jacob arose and took his stone pillow and poured oil over it and set it as a reminder to the whole world that God had been there.

Then Jacob made a promise to God. "If God will watch over me on this journey and I return safely to my father's house, then Yahweh the Lord will be my God and I will give Him a tenth of all I may own."

Affirmation: I know the Lord is watching over me!

THE PSALM OF THE SHEPHERD KING DAVID

Psalm 23:1 The Lord is my shepherd; I shall not want.

The Lord is my shepherd, I shall not want.
He makes me to lie down in green pastures.
He leads me beside the still waters.
He restores my soul.
He leads me in the paths of righteousness
  for His name's sake.
Yea though I walk through the valley of the shadow of death,
I will fear no evil, for You are with me.
Your rod and Your staff, they comfort me.
You prepare a table before me
  in the presence of my enemies.
You anoint my head with oil.
My cup runs over.
Surely goodness and mercy shall follow me
  all the days of my life,
And I will dwell in the house of the
  Lord forever.

Affirmation: I will trust the Lord, my Shepherd!

THE SECOND LAW

Deuteronomy 6:5 (You shall) Love the Lord your God with all your heart,... soul,... (and) strength.

Moses continued to teach the word of the Lord to the children of Israel. He spoke these beautiful words: "Hear, O Israel. The Lord our God, the Lord is one. You shall love the Lord your God with all your heart, soul, and strength."

"Think about His commandments every day. Teach them to your children. Talk about them when you are sitting at home or away from home. Even before you close your eyes at night, remember God's goodness."

"Fear the Lord and serve Him only. Do not be persuaded by your friends to disobey the Lord, for this is not pleasing to the Lord. Keep His commandments and love Him always." Moses taught the people of Israel how to live a godly life.

After many years of traveling and learning about God, the children of Israel were now ready to enter the land God had promised them. Joshua was appointed to lead the people into the promised land.

As the people prepared to cross the Jordan River into the promised land, Moses spoke to them one last time. "Remember the greatness of our God. Obey His commands and you will be a great nation." Then he sang a praise hymn to the Lord.

Moses climbed up the high mountain called Nebo, and the Lord showed Moses the land promised to Abraham, Isaac, and Jacob. He could see the city of Jericho all the way to the sea.

After Moses had seen this, he died and was received into heaven. The people of Israel were very sad Moses had died, for he was a great man of God.

Affirmation: I am thankful for God's goodness!

ISAIAH SEES THE FUTURE

Isaiah 43:5   Fear ... not; for I am with (you).

The nation of Israel had once again fallen deep into sin. They had rebelled against the Lord and chosen a wicked way of living.

There arose a prophet of God named Isaiah, who came to proclaim God's coming judgments on Israel and upon the whole earth. He told them that God would not allow their sin to go unpunished.

"Clean your minds," Isaiah proclaimed. "Make yourselves a holy people. Repent and stop doing evil things. Learn to do good! And though your sins be as scarlet, they shall be washed whiter than snow."

Isaiah taught the people to stop calling bad things good, and good things bad. "Have faith," he said, "and follow the Lord even when His ways are unclear to you. Respect the Lord and trust in Him. For there is no salvation in knowing about God. You must pray and spend time with God. And know this above all things: God loves you," he said, "and though we are very small, God cares for us."

Isaiah was a prophet, a person with a message from God. Isaiah's message was not only about the past and the present, but also about the future. Hundreds of years before Jesus was born, Isaiah wrote of His birth and His death. God had allowed him to see into the future.

"For unto us a child (Jesus) is born, unto us a son is given. And He alone will establish a kingdom. And He will be called Wonderful Counselor, Mighty God, Everlasting Father, The Prince Of Peace."

Isaiah also wrote of Jesus' death:

"He (Jesus) was despised and rejected by men. He took upon himself our sins and sorrows. He was pierced because of the sinful deeds we had done. He took the punishment we deserved and because of this, we are forgiven. For everyone is guilty of sinning, but Jesus has been punished in our place ... though He had done nothing wrong."

The Lord spoke many wonderful things through the prophet Isaiah.

Affirmation: I will serve Jesus, the Prince of Peace!

HE PROMISES TO LOVE US

John 14:21 Whoever has my commands and obeys them, he is the one who loves me. He who loves me will be loved by my Father, and I too will love him and show myself to him.

John writes; Jesus taught His followers many lessons about love. We are to love our neighbor as ourself. We are to love God and Jesus promises to love us! He said, "Anyone who loves Me will be loved by My Heavenly Father and I will show them love too!" How do we show Jesus we love Him? Jesus said, "If anyone loves Me, they will obey My teachings."

*Affirmation:
I will obey Jesus!*

HE PROMISES TO GUIDE US

John 14:6   Jesus answered, "I am the way and the truth and the life. No one comes to the Father except through me."

One day Thomas, a disciple of Jesus, asked Him a very important question. "Lord, how can we know which way to go?" Jesus answered, "I am the Way and the Truth and the Life. No one comes to our Heavenly Father without first finding forgiveness in Me." If we follow the teachings of Jesus found in the Bible and pray, we will be on the right path!

Affirmation: I will follow Jesus!

HE PROMISES TO PROTECT US

John 10:11   I am the good shepherd. The good shepherd lays down his life for the sheep.

John writes; Jesus once said that we are like sheep and He was the Good Shepherd. Sheep do not know which way to go, so they listen for the Good Shepherd's voice and follow. Sheep never follow a stranger's voice; in fact, they run away from strangers. Jesus said, "I am the Good Shepherd, and the good shepherd is ready to die protecting His sheep." Jesus loves you and He will take care of you!

Affirmation: Jesus will take care of me!

HE PROMISES TO COMFORT US

John 14:1-2   Do not let your hearts be troubled. Trust in God; trust also in me. In my Father's house are many rooms; if it were not so, I would have told you. I am going there to prepare a place for you.

Jesus said, "Do not let your hearts be troubled. Don't be filled with sorrow and sadness. Trust in God, for He is able to comfort you. Trust also in Me, for you have so much to look forward to! Keep your eyes fixed on heaven, for I'm going there to prepare a place just for you."

Affirmation: I will trust Jesus to comfort me!

HE PROMISES TO SEND THE HOLY SPIRIT

John 14:16-17a   And I will ask the Father, and he will give you another Counselor to be with you forever - the Spirit of truth.

Jesus said that if we love Him, we will obey His commandments. He said, "I will ask My Heavenly Father, and He will send the Holy Spirit to those who love God. He will walk with you and guide you each and every day, and He will teach you all things and will remind you of everything I have said to you."

Affirmation: I will walk with the Holy Spirit!

HE PROMISES TO ANSWER PRAYER

John 16:24   Until now you have not asked for anything in my name. Ask and you will receive, and your joy will be complete.

Jesus taught His followers to pray. Prayer is talking to God. And since God is our dearest and closest friend, we should talk to Him every day.

Does God answer our prayers? Jesus said, "I tell you the truth, My Heavenly Father will give you whatever you ask for in prayer if you ask in My name." This means we should pray for things that would please Jesus.

Affirmation: I will pray for things that please Jesus!

HE PROMISES US ETERNAL LIFE

***John 3:16** For God so loved the world, that He gave His only begotten Son.*

How long do most people live? Some live to be 70 years old, some 80, a few even 100 years old. The greatest promise of all in the Bible is the one Jesus made in John 3:16.

"For God so loved the world (that means you and me) that He gave His only begotten Son (that's Jesus!) that whosoever believes in Him should not perish (that means they will never die), but have everlasting life." If we love God, someday we will live with Jesus in heaven forever!

Affirmation: I want to go to heaven!

COLLECT ALL 10

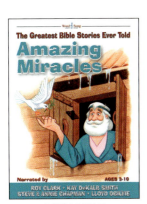
0-8054-2471-7

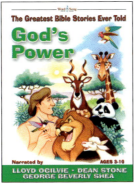
0-8054-2466-0

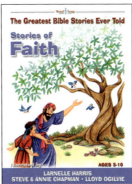
0-8054-2470-9

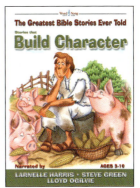
0-8054-2469-5

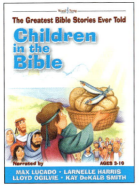
0-8054-2474-1

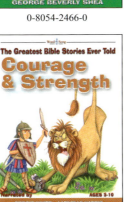
0-8054-2468-7

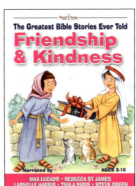
0-8054-2473-3

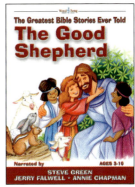
0-8054-2475-x

0-8054-2472-5

Available in Your Favorite Christian Bookstore.

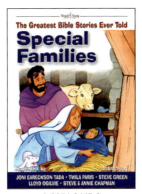
0-8054-2467-9

We hope you enjoyed this Word & Song Storybook.